HAL•LEONARD

GUITAR
PLAY-ALONG®

VOL. 170

T0055797

CONTENTS

Cover photo: Scott Legato/Getty Images

ISBN 978-1-4803-3171-6

HAL•LEONARD®
CORPORATION
7777 W. BLUEMOUND RD. P.O. BOX 13819 MILWAUKEE, WI 53213

In Australia Contact:
Hal Leonard Australia Pty. Ltd.
4 Lentara Court
Cheltenham, Victoria, 3192 Australia
Email: ausadmin@halleonard.com.au

Visit Hal Leonard Online at
www.halleonard.com

Animal I Have Become

Words and Music by Three Days Grace, Gavin Brown and Barry Stock

Drop D tuning, down 1 step:
(low to high) C-G-C-F-A-D

Intro

Moderately ♩ = 123

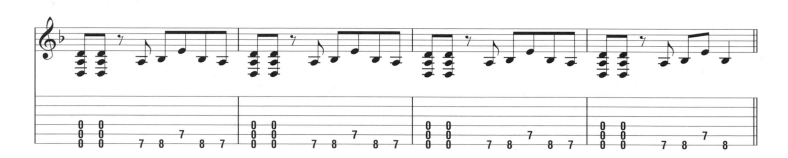

Verse

1. I can't es-cape this ___ hell. ___

So man-y times ___ I've ___ tried, ___

Some-bod-y help me tame this an-i-mal I have be-come. Help me be-lieve

it's not the real __ me. Some-bod-y help me tame this an-i-

Outro

mal. _____ This an-i-mal I have be-

come.

Chalk Outline

Words and Music by Three Days Grace, Barry Stock and Craig Wiseman

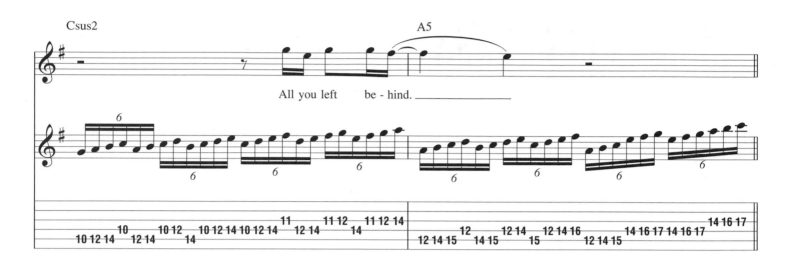

Chorus

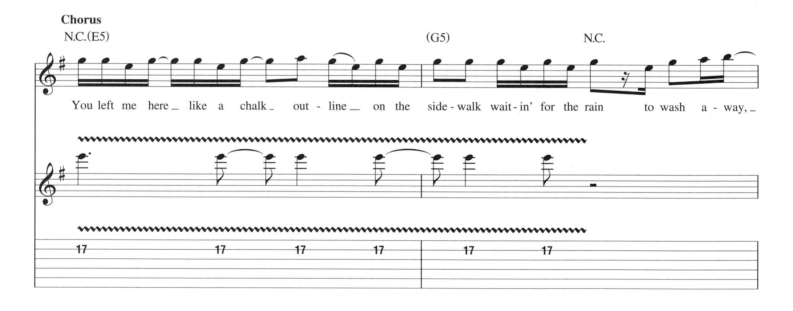

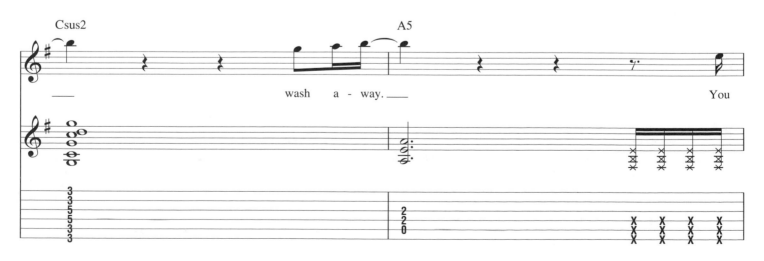

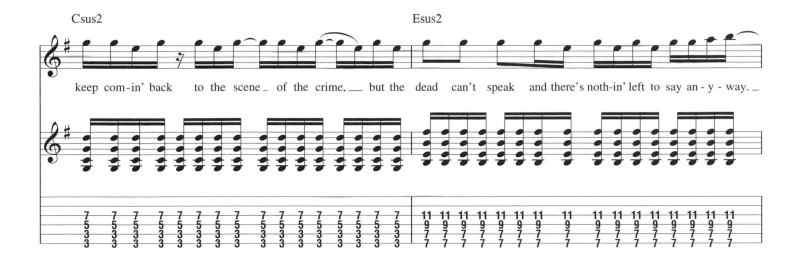

keep com-in' back to the scene of the crime, but the dead can't speak and there's noth-in' left to say an-y-way.

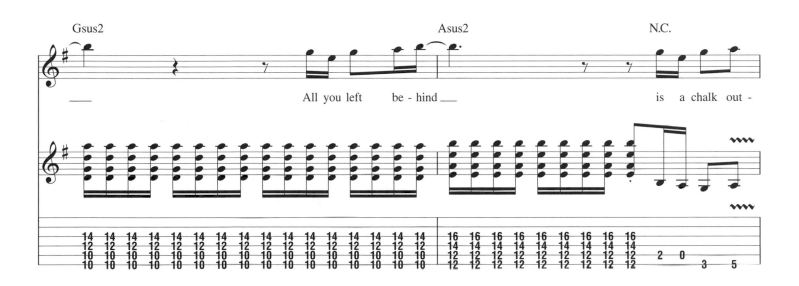

All you left be-hind is a chalk out-

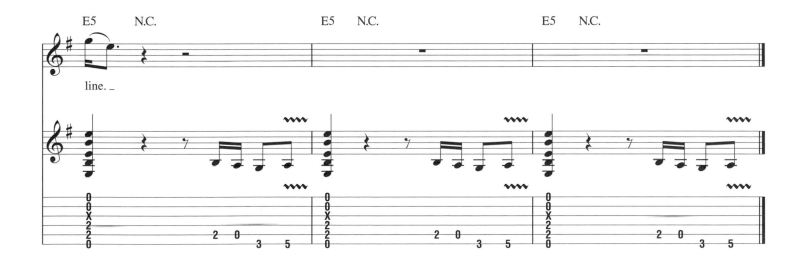

line.

Additional Lyrics

2. I've been cold in the crypt,
But not as cold as the words across your lips.
You'll be sorry, baby, someday,
When you reach across the bed where my body used to lay.

The Good Life

Words and Music by Three Days Grace and Barry Stock

Drop D tuning:
(low to high) D-A-D-G-B-E

Intro
Moderately ♩ = 128

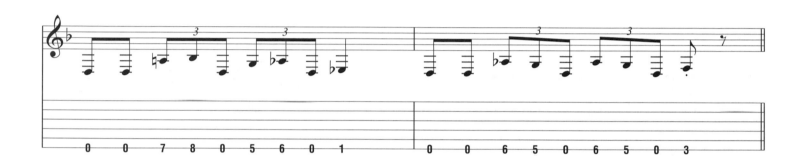

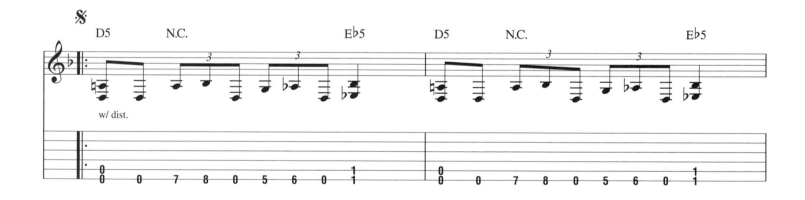

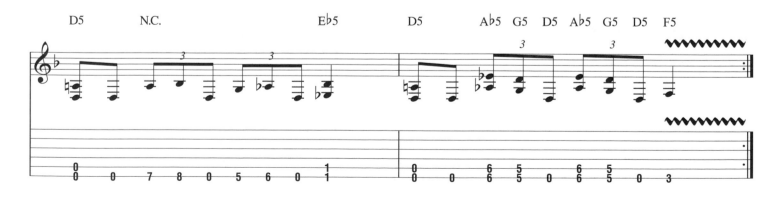

Verse

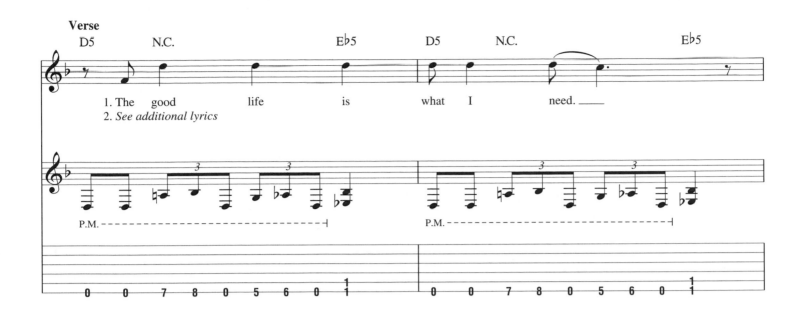

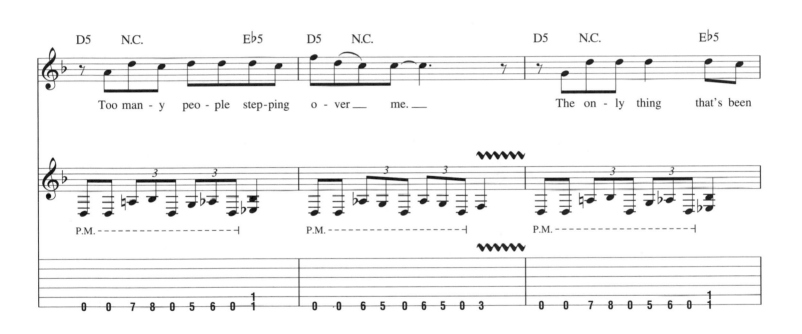

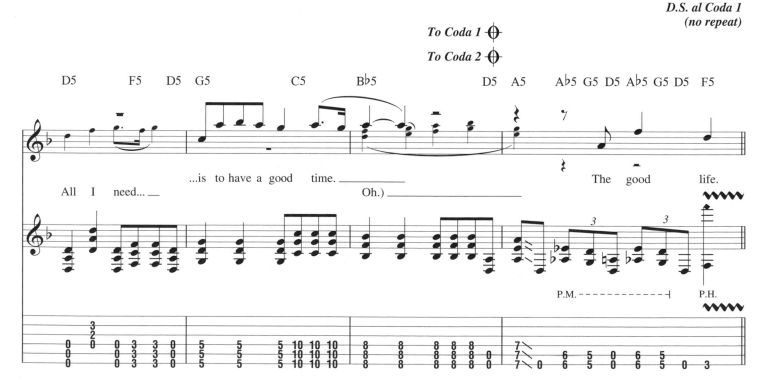

Additional Lyrics

2. I don't really know who I am.
   It's time for me to take a stand.
   I need a change and I need it fast.
   I know that any day could be the last.

Never Too Late

Words and Music by Three Days Grace and Gavin Brown

Additional Lyrics

2. No one will ever see this side reflected.
   And if there's something wrong, who would've guessed it?
   And I have left alone ev'rything that I own
   To make you feel like it's not too late. It's never too late.

I Hate Everything About You

Words and Music by Three Days Grace and Gavin Brown

Drop D tuning:
(low to high) D-A-D-G-B-E

Intro
Fast Rock ♩ = 168

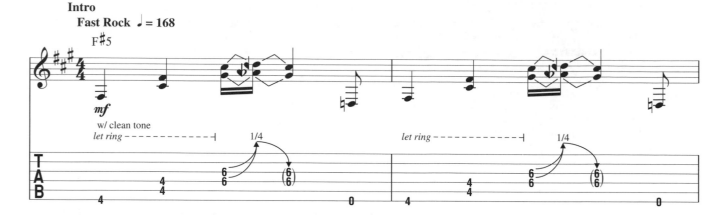

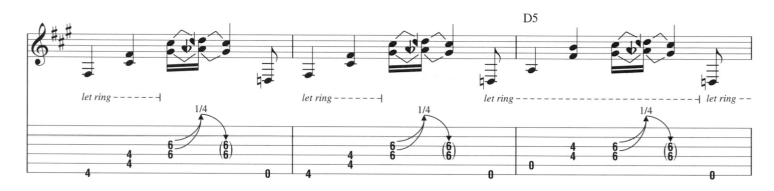

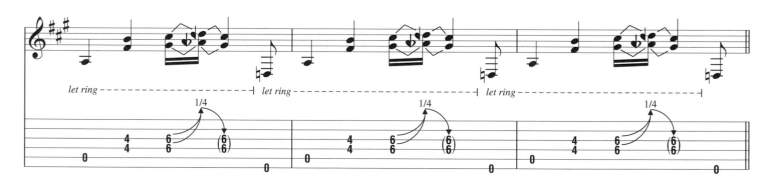

Verse

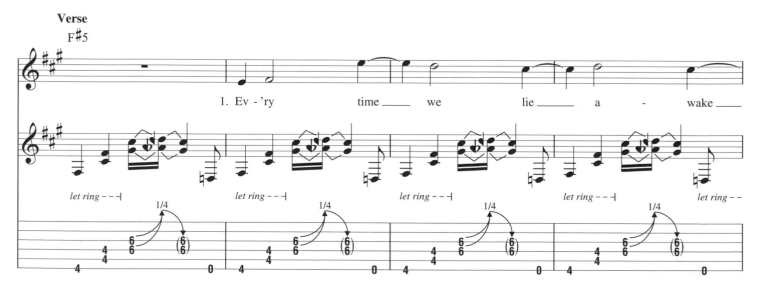

1. Ev-'ry   time   we   lie   a-   wake

Pre-Chorus

26

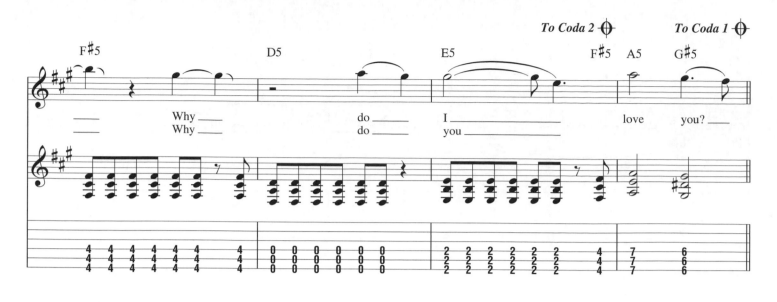

Why ___ do ___ I ___ love you? ___
Why ___ do ___ you ___

Interlude

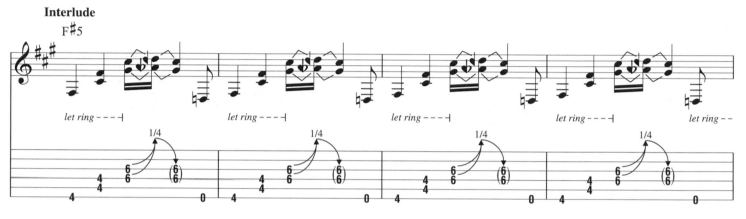

Verse

2. Ev - 'ry time ___ we lie ___ a - wake ___

D.S. al Coda 1

Interlude

D.S.S. al Coda 2

Just Like You

Words and Music by Three Days Grace and Gavin Brown

Drop D tuning, down 1/2 step:
(low to high) Db-Ab-Db-Gb-Bb-Eb

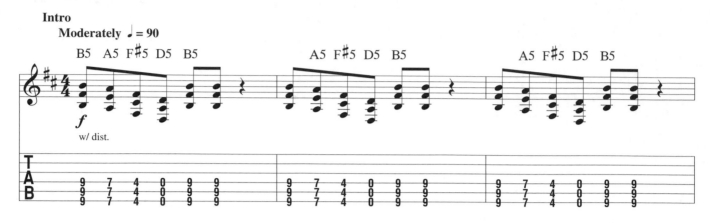

Additional Lyrics

2. I could be cold. I could be ruthless.
   You know I could be just like you.
   I could be weak. I could be senseless.
   You know I could be just like you.

Riot

Words and Music by Three Days Grace and Barry Stock

Drop D tuning, down 1 step:
(low to high) C-G-C-F-A-D

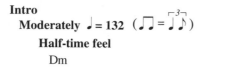

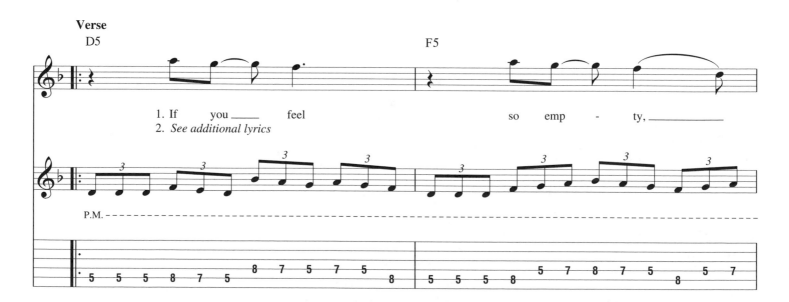

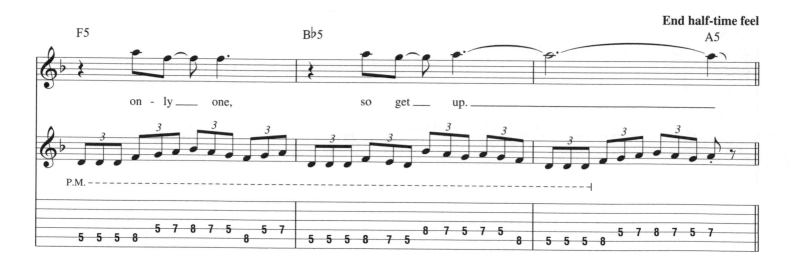

Interlude

Additional Lyrics

2. If you feel so filthy, so dirty, so fucked up,
   If you feel so walked on, so painful, so pissed off,
   You're not the only one refusing to go down.
   You're not the only one, so get up.

Pain

Words and Music by Three Days Grace, Gavin Brown and Barry Stock

Drop D tuning:
(low to high) D-A-D-G-B-E

Intro
Moderately slow ♩ = 81

Verse

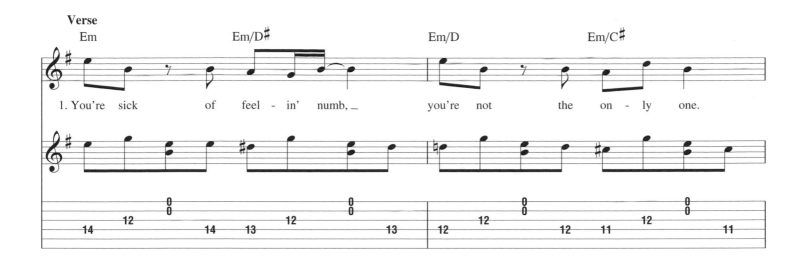

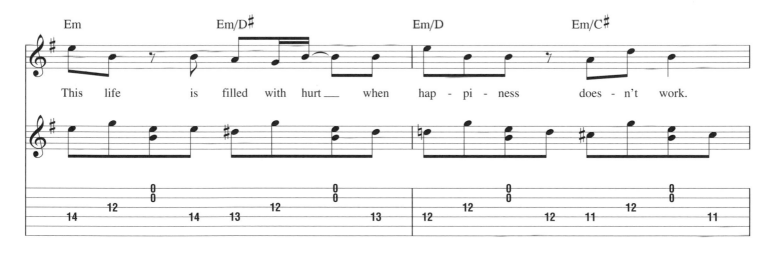

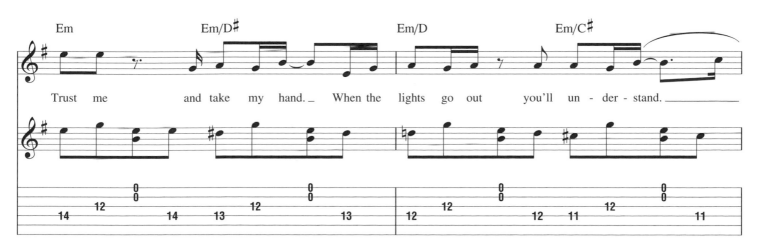

To Coda

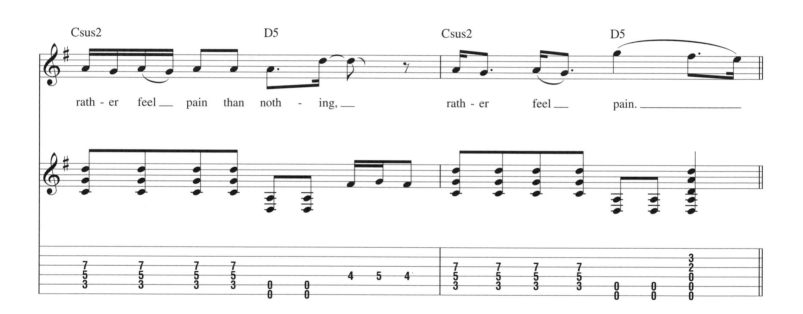

Bridge

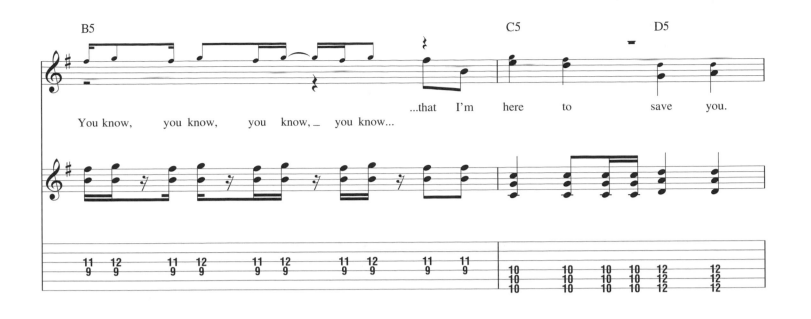

You know,   you know,   you know,_ you know...

...that I'm here to save you.

You know,   you know,   you know,_ you know...

...I'm al - ways here   for _____ you.

I know,   I know,   I know,_ I know...)

...that you'll thank me   lat - er. _____

Interlude

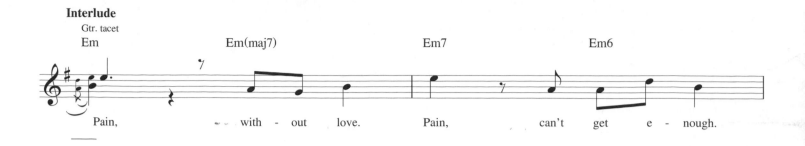

Pain, — with - out love. Pain, can't get e - nough.

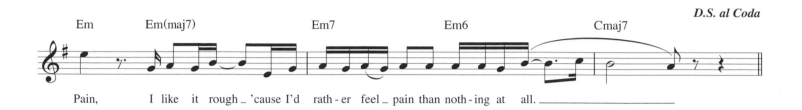

Pain, I like it rough — 'cause I'd rath - er feel — pain than noth - ing at all. _____

⊕ Coda

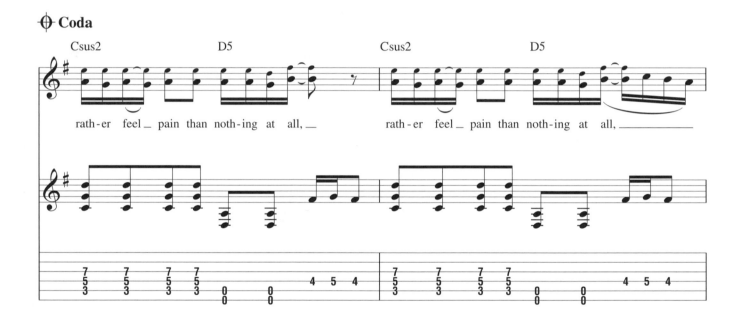

rath - er feel — pain than noth - ing at all, — rath - er feel — pain than noth - ing at all, _____

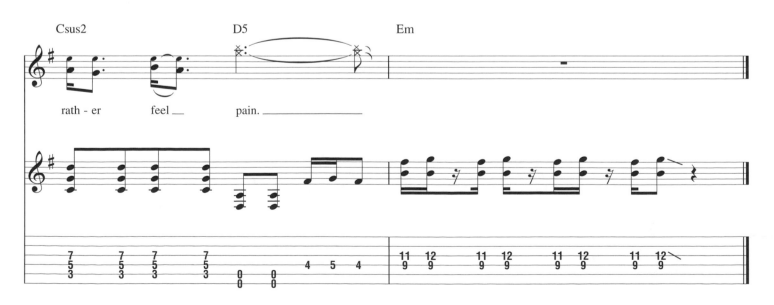

rath - er feel — pain. _____